THE PEACEABLE KINGDOM

David Hazard

Decorations by *Ferrandiz*

Published by
Chosen Books, Lincoln, Virginia 22078
of the Zondervan Corporation
Grand Rapids, Michigan 49506

THE PEACEABLE KINGDOM
Copyright © 1982, David Hazard
Illustrations © ANRI AG, St., Christina, Italy

Library of Congress Cataloging in Publication Data
Hazard, David
    The peaceable kingdom.

    Summary:
    Stories, songs, and poems about the
    inhabitants of a fanciful kingdom, with
    a Christian emphasis.

    1. Children's literature, American
[1. Literature—Collections 2. Christian life—Literary Collections].
I. Ferrándiz, ill. II. Title.
PZ7.H314967Pe   1983   [Fic]   82-23531
ISBN 0301-605-20-2

All rights reserved. No part of this publication may be reproduced, stored in a retrieval system, or transmitted in any form or by any means without the prior permission of the publisher.

Printed in the United States of America.

Chosen Books is a division of The Zondervan Corporation, Grand Rapids, Michigan 49506. Editorial offices for Chosen Books are in Lincoln, Virginia 22078

To MaryLynne,
my treasured friend in the Peaceable Kingdom

*Instead of the thorn
the myrtle will grow.*

ACKNOWLEDGEMENTS

I am deeply grateful to Juan Ferrandiz Castells for inspiring this book. His love for children and the Spirit of his gifted artwork are the well-spring of these stories. The poem, *Under God's Canopy*, is dedicated to him.

Special thanks: to Ernst Riffeser, President of ANRI, where Ferrandiz' artwork is translated into the exquisite wood-carvings which appear in this book; to Paul Schmid III for his enthusiasm and support; to William Lee for his musical advice; and to Ann Cherryman for her design artistry.

THE
PEACEABLE KINGDOM

CONTENTS

The Kingdom Where the World Begins
9

Butter and the Egg Girl
19

The Spring Dance
25

The Tale of A Bird
26

A Secret to Tell
36

A Star In the Night
37

Under God's Canopy
48

Small Angel ran ahead of me up a billowy hill of clouds. In my chase, I slid down the north wind and tripped on the tail of shooting star. A mountain poked its head through the clouds, and we ran right out of the sky onto a grassy meadow.

"Where are we?" I gasped, stopping to catch my breath.

"We're in The Peaceable Kingdom," Small Angel smiled. "It's my favorite place. There are stories and songs here and—well, let's sit down and listen."

I laid my head in a tuft of spearmint and red saxifrage, and the wind began to whisper . . .

THE KINGDOM
WHERE THE WORLD BEGINS

On the tip of a mountain, so high up it disappeared above swirling clouds, stood a house of stone. A King lived there and he had one son.

Outside their back door grew a very old garden. Here the trees linked arms overhead like children in a dance. There were banks of thorny red roses, bluebells, harebells, Maybells and purple, magic-smelling irises and one very old tree. Up from the tree's roots spouted a stream—clear, quick and cold.

The stone house and the garden remained a secret for a long time. Until one day a girl named Ribbon came wandering up the mountain.

The morning sun was rising like a yellow bubble in the blue pool of the sky. Ribbon was lost. The flowers smelled so sweet they had lured her far beyond the fields she knew. And then she found the stream, with its voice so musical it washed away all her fear of being lost.

Rippling over a bed of smooth stones, the water sang:

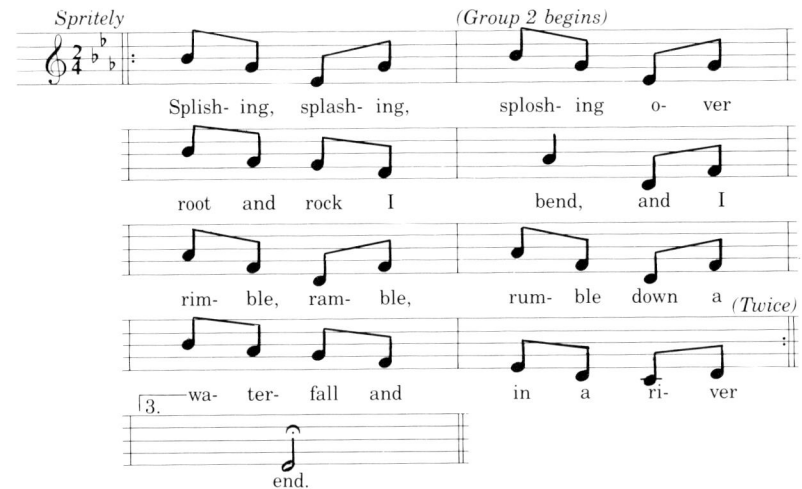

Ribbon followed the stream up—up past the clouds that gathered like white sheep grazing on the mountainside. Near the very top, she came upon the stone house. Beyond was a garden, and the musical stream flowed out from under its leafy green canopy.

"I wonder who lives here," Ribbon said out loud. (She often spoke to herself when she was alone, don't you?)

"I live here—with my father, the King." A boy, just about Ribbon's age, was sitting up in a tree. He swung down and dropped with a *plop* at her feet. "My name is Prince Song," he said. "And your name is Ribbon, isn't it?"

Ribbon frowned, "How do you know my name?"

"Father knows most everything. He told me you'd be coming today."

"But I didn't *mean* to come here. It was an accident—I got lost," she replied.

"Here in the Peaceable Kingdom nothing happens by accident," the prince laughed. "You were meant to come. Anyway, I'm glad you're here."

Ribbon felt as if she were in a fairytale—and it felt very nice. She asked: "Does the stream begin here in your garden?"

"Yes," said the prince, and he took her hand as if they'd always been friends. "I'll show you."

Through the garden they walked, between the mounds of sweet flowers, until the path spread into a clearing. In the center stood a tree, with bark as wrinkly as an old man's face. A spring gushed up from its roots and slid away on a slate-bed. Sunlight danced like diamonds on the water.

"How beautiful," breathed Ribbon. "The whole world must begin right here!"

Prince Song dipped his finger in the flowing stream and lifted out a bubble. Round and crystally it spun on the tip of his finger.

"Watch this," he winked at Ribbon. In a clear voice he sang: "From the tree root springs the water. From the water springs the bird . . ."

As she watched, the bubble twitched and grew and all at once became a fluttering bird. Lightly, the prince set it on Ribbon's finger.

"How did you do that?" she marvelled. "Can I try it?"

"Of course! Just catch some bubbles."

Ribbon dipped her hand in the water and caught three bubbles. She thought for a moment, then sang: "From the tree root springs the water. From the water comes—umm—two rabbits and another bird."

It wasn't sung in rhythm, but it worked. Two furry rabbits sniffed at her with whiskery noses, and a second bird sat ruffling and stretching its wings.

"Let's make more!" Ribbon said, giggling.

And so they passed the entire morning, singing and creating animals from the stream's marvelous bubbles. They made birds, mice, lambs, a cat and a dog, rabbits, a goose and a turtle, a goat and many other animals.

After a time, the prince said, "Come on, Ribbon. I want to show you the rest of the garden."

And to the animals, he gave a stern warning. "You're safe here in the Peaceable Kingdom. Don't go down into the kingdom of the world. You'd be in great danger."

"Oh, we won't leave," said the dog, wagging his head and his tail. "We promise!" said the others.

As Ribbon and Prince Song disappeared down the path, the cat twitched her tail.

"Watch me!" she purred. And she stepped out onto the rushing stream—just like an ice-skater on top of the water. There she stood on its glassy ripples.

"Let me try that!" cried the others. With a hop! slip! flap! they followed. And away they slid, skating and scooting down the mountain.

For a long time they laughed and tumbled and scooted along. Suddenly, the turtle looked about and saw they had drifted into a valley of gloomy shadows.

"I wonder where we are," he said in a voice, as slow and thick as mud.

They all slid off the stream just at the edge of a deep-furrowed field where a small, gray donkey stood looking very sad.

"Excuse me, sir," the mother rabbit snuffled. "We're from the Peaceable Kingdom. Whose land is this?"

The donkey's weary shoulders sagged. He whispered: "Don't stop here. This land belongs to the Master of Night. He forces me to work for him with a cruel whip that stings."

Behind a hillock of trees, wrapped in his dark cloak, the Master of Night was listening. He had hated Prince Song and his father for so long that he could not even remember why. From his dark pouch, he drew a net made of ropes.

The goat was saying, "May-ay-ay-be we can help the donkey escape from here."

Suddenly a thick net flew over their heads. Only the goose escaped, flapping away up the stream.

The Master of Night called after him, "Go tell Prince Song I've captured his unruly friends. They belong to me now."

The animals in the net said nothing, for they had fallen into a deep sleep.

U̲p on the mountain, Ribbon and the prince had wandered back to the spring again. The sun was now sliding toward the evening edge of the world.

In a great fluster, the goose flew up. "Prince Song! Song! Song!" he honked, "the Master of Night has caught all the others in his net. Oh, I wish we'd never left the garden."

"Who is the Master of Night?" Ribbon asked.

"He used to tend the garden," the prince answered gravely. "But he became wicked. Father drove him out into the kingdom of the world. We have to go and free the animals or he may hurt them."

As he spoke, the prince stepped out right on top of the stream. He reached for Ribbon's hand and she stepped out on the water, too. But her feet flew up. She fell, and landed without a splash, bouncing like a bubble.

The goose sat down at her side, and together they glided along on the water. Smooth and fast was the ride as they flowed past the mountain meadows.

Suddenly, the prince cried: "Hold on tight! Here we go-oo-oo-oo . . ." and over a waterfall they dropped. Ribbon felt all twizzly and tickly, as if her stomach were full of feathers. At the bottom, the stream rushed on, crisping and twinkling in the late sun.

The sky was very dark when they reached the valley. The goose waddled up the bank of the stream honking, "Donkey! Donkey! There's the donkey."

He was hard at work, pulling a wagon-load of heavy boulders. Ribbon stroked his hot forelock, and the boy said, "I'm Prince Song. Where has your master taken our friends?"

The donkey looked up at the darkening sky. "We'll have to hurry, the night has almost come," he brayed. "Loose my harness and I'll lead the way."

Over the fields they trotted, with the goose flapping along after. The moon rose, a gold crescent pouring shadows everywhere.

"My master has bound your friends in the deepest, coldest reaches of his power," the donkey said as they ran. "They're asleep on the hill, as silent as stones—even their breath is still. All the power in the world cannot set them free."

"You're right," said the prince, with a mysterious smile. "But maybe one song will wake them!"

The hill loomed before them, gray and still and eerie in the moonlight. Up the slope they climbed, and Ribbon felt as if the darkness were full of peering eyes.

I suppose that you have seen an animal sleeping, curled up in its warm fur coat. The animals of the Peaceable Kingdom did not look at all warm and furry now. At the top of the hill, they stood frozen in a ring. Their cold, lifeless eyes made Ribbon shiver.

"Be quick," whispered the donkey.

Prince Song reached into his pouch and drew out a flute. Standing in the ring of silent animals, he began to play—very softly at first. The voice of the flute was lovely and wooden, tender as the call of a lark. Flitting and trilling, it climbed the night air.

Ribbon began to drift into sleep in a wonderful dream of sunshine and musical, laughing water. Prince Song came riding down her dream on a stream of light. He moved in and out of a circle of stones, blowing on them with his warm breath. Each stone he passed melted, as ice melts into water. And the sound of laughter grew louder and louder . . .

Ribbon woke with the moonlight in her eyes. The donkey was nuzzling her ear. "The prince has set our friends free," he said, prancing.

Ribbon was so happy to see her friends, warm and alive once more, and she was about to join in the dance. And then they were startled by an angry voice.

"Thief! I caught these animals in my kingdom. Leave them to me, and go back to your own kingdom, Prince Song!"

The Master of Night was rushing toward them up the hill. In his hand, he swung the thick net of ropes.

"He'll catch us all!" Ribbon cried, huddling against the prince. The animals crouched low, trembling.

Prince Song only chuckled. "His power is broken. You don't have to be afraid of the darkness any more."

Even as he spoke, a strange thing was happening. The Master of Night grew smaller and further away, even though he was still rushing toward them up the hill.

Ribbon felt giddy and light-headed. Looking down, she saw that she, the prince, all the animals were no longer standing on the hill. They were rising through the night sky, spinning and twirling like a flock of bubbles. She felt a warm breeze, and turned to see that Prince Song was puffing at them, lifting them upward.

The sleepy moon sank beneath their feet, and soon the sky grew lighter. They landed in the prince's garden on the mountain just as the morning sun rose.

"We're home, in the kingdom where the world begins!" shouted the animals. "We'll never disobey and wander away again."

Prince Song again drew out his flute. "Let's have a celebration dance. Will you help me make some music, Ribbon?"

"Yes," she replied. And soon the garden was filled with songs and the risen sun.

BUTTER AND THE EGG GIRL

One bright, beautiful, billowy day, Ribbon went walking through the Peaceable Kingdom. The wonderful stream was bubbling in its bed of stones and watering the garden.

She walked until she was tired, and was about to sit down on a brown, odd-looking clump of earth.

"Don't sit on me!" cried the clump. Ribbon was so startled that she slipped and fell on the grass.

"Oh, I'm sorry," Ribbon apologized. "Who are you?"

The clump turned about very slowly until she could see two eyes above a flat bill and four webbed feet. "I'm the platypus," he said, in a quackery voice.

"Why are you sitting here all alone?" she asked.

"Because I'm—I'm *different* from the other animals. I look and act and sound different. I don't think they like me. Some days I wish I was somebody else."

Ribbon took him on her lap. "Listen," she said, stroking his funny little head, "I know a story that will help you feel better. This is how it goes."

Once there was an enormous egg. No one knew where it came from, but there it was.

Down a grassy hill it bumped, tumbling and toppling, rolling and wobbling. With a *whack* and a *crack*, the egg struck a rock and stopped, resting in a patch of bright flowers.

Nearby, some new-hatched chicks were pecking about in the sunny meadow. They scurried through the grass, peeping, "See! See! See the strange, enormous, funny egg!"

One little chick hopped up on the smooth white shell and cried, "It's moving!"

And slowly the eggshell crack-ack-acked open. Out came a finger, an arm, then a pretty little girl's face. She had laughing eyes and a sweet, pink mouth like a bow.

"Oh, that ride made me dizzy," she chuckled to the chicks. Then she stretched her arms. "What a beautiful day to be born."

As she sat looking out across the green hills, a boy came wandering through the flowers.

"What are you?" he asked with a frown.

"I'm not a *what*," replied the girl. "I'm a *who*. I am somebody, and my name is Eglantine. *Who* are you?"

But the boy didn't answer. He stepped back, staring at her silently and frowning all the while. Then he spoke gruffly.

"Eglantine—what a funny name. And how strange to be born in an egg. I don't think I like you."

Eglantine felt a prickle of sadness in her heart. "But what's your name?" she asked, still trying to be friendly. "And where are you going?"

The boy was already walking away through the sunny grass. "My name is Butter," he called over his shoulder. "And I'm going off to invite my friends to a special party. We're having cake and ice cream and toffee and games—but you're not invited. You're *different*—not like the rest of us."

Eglantine sat in a gloomy silence as she watched Butter disappear into a pine forest. Then she climbed out of her eggshell and sat down on the grass. The chicks scurried onto her lap.

"Am I *bad* because I was born in an egg?" she asked them. "Is it wrong to be different?"

"Oh no," they peeped. "We hatched out of eggs, too. And you're just like us—well, almost."

And to cheer her up, they played catching games together far into the day. When they got hungry, the chicks scratched in the dirt for worms to eat—which made Eglantine's stomach uneasy. Sitting down to rest on a fallen log, she found that the bees had left a honeycomb inside, so she ate it for her supper.

The stars had popped out like daisies in the evening sky, as she licked her sticky fingers.

"I'm so sleepy," she yawned. "Time to curl up in my eggshell."

But the shell was now much too small. Eglantine could not get herself inside no matter how she squashed up or drew in her knees. She stood beside it, puzzling.

"The shell didn't get smaller," said the chicks. "You've gotten bigger. You're growing up fast, just as we are. In a short time, we'll be hens and roosters."

"But where will I spend the night?" sniffed Eglantine.

"We'd take you home with us," replied the chicks, "but you're too big to sleep under Mother's wings."

So Eglantine was left alone on the hillside for the night. She lay down and drew a coverlet of clover blossoms over her to keep away the night breeze.

"I wonder if I'll always be *different* from everyone else," she sighed. "I'm not like other children—and I certainly won't grow up to be a hen or a rooster. So what will I be?" And she slipped into a silver sleep.

The very next day, Butter was busy once again inviting friends to his special party. He had just left his home in the pine forest when he met two girls, Kerchief and Curl, gathering mushrooms in their baskets.

"Can you come to my party?" he asked.

"Oh, yes," they replied with delight. "May we invite our friends?"

"Sure," said Butter. Then he leaned close and whispered, "But don't invite the girl in the egg. She's *different* from us."

And off he ran through the forest. Along the way, he met four boys—String, Milkshake, Thistle and Shoe—going to the swimming hole. And he invited them, too.

"But don't invite the girl in the egg," he whispered. "She's *different.*"

Soon Butter had invited everyone around. He hurried home to prepare for his party. He baked acorn cakes, pickle pies and dozens of cookies. He made elephant ice cream and sweet, sticky toffee. He planned games and contests and races. For days and days and days he worked.

At long, long last, the party day dawned. Butter was up with the first rays of the sun, full of excitement. But he waited and waited, and still no one knocked at his door.

"Maybe they all forgot," he mumbled, feeling a little blue. "I'd better go find them."

Butter searched through the forest, but found no one. At last, he met them in the open field—Kerchief, Curl, String, Milkshake, Thistle and Shoe—and all the other party guests.

Curl ran up when she saw him. "Oh, Butter, I'm sorry we're all so late for your party. But we've just met the nicest, friendliest, most wonderful person. She's different from the rest of us. May we invite her?"

Standing in the midst of Butter's friends was the loveliest person he'd ever seen. Her face glowed, and at her back were strong, beautiful wings.

"Hello, Butter," she said timidly. "I was the little girl in the egg. But look what I've become. I have beautiful wings."

Butter's face was red with embarrassment. "I—I'm sorry that I was rude to you. I thought that you were bad just because you were different."

"I am different," said Eglantine with a beaming smile. "I'm special. I was born in an egg because I was meant to fly."

With that, she handed him a basket of bright, glittering stars. "They are decorations for your party," she smiled.

Then they all went to Butter's house. Eglantine was the very special guest. She flew Butter and each of his friends up and over the prickly pine branches, high above the owl's nest. They had a wonderful party—now that everyone was there.

When Ribbon finished the story, the platypus was still sitting on her lap looking very thoughtful.

Ribbon stroked his head and said, "You see, nobody else looks or acts or sounds like you because you're *special*. And besides all that, I like you."

"Do you? Do you like me?" asked the platypus, and his wide bill turned up in a smile. "Oh, I enjoyed your story very much. But when someone says they like you—well, that's the very best thing of all."

"Let's go see the other animals," said Ribbon, "and we'll have a party."

And that's just what they did.

THE SPRING DANCE

The mountains and hills have burst into singing
the trees in the fields all clap and prance,
and joy flows out like streams a-bubbling—
Come and join me in the dance.

I dance like water, circling, singing,
I dance like wind in the tree,
for I'm happy that God made hills and rivers
and I'm happy that God made me.

THE TALE OF A BIRD

Rain drizzled down the window panes of the Peaceable Kingdom. The cat was curled in a soft armchair close by the fire. She yawned a fangful yawn, stretched her claws and sat up.

"I suppose you'd like to hear a story," she said, in a voice like warm milk, "since it's gray and wet outdoors, and all your friends are at home.

"I know just the right story for a day like today. Come a bit closer, and don't sit on my tail, if you please."

And her whiskers tickled as she whis-purrred in my ear:

In a cottage in the mountains at the edge of the world, a boy named Applecheek lived with his mother and father. He was always lonely. There were no other children to climb and swim and run with barefoot through the open fields. No one—except Ruckus.

Ruckus lived beyond the oak forest. He was a loud and rough boy, and Applecheek didn't like him. He crept through the forest and startled the deer so they bounded away in white-eyed terror. He threw stones in the brook till the minnows spun in mad circles.

So Applecheek kept to himself, but every day he wished for a friend.

On the first Spring morning, robins were singing outside his window:

Applecheek ran out into the sun-shiny morning. The first warm fingers of light were touching the mountains. Rocky peaks took off their white snow robes. Yellow jonquils trumpeted across the high meadows. In the brook, little frogs "peeped" like tiny silver bells on the wind.

He searched the trees, but the robins had already flown off to gather food for their chicks. "There's no one to play with today," said Applecheek glumly to no one at all. "And there was no one to play with yesterday—or the day before."

Feeling very sorry for himself, he scuffed off through the shaded oak forest. He hadn't walked very far before he heard scuffling just beyond some thick, green-budding bushes. A very confused voice was jabbering:

"Wap your flings! I mean, bap your smings. Oh, bejabbers. I mean, *flap your wings!*"

Peeking through the bushes, he saw two rabbits—one gray and the other brown. The gray rabbit was standing on top of the brown one's head, holding a baby bird high into the air. With much wobbling and "get-off-my-ear" complaints, they were trying to teach the poor little bird how to fly.

Applecheek stepped timidly from the bushes. "Can I help?" he offered.

"Yeeowwee!" Brown Rabbit hollered, hopping a foot into the air. Gray Rabbit toppled off his head, and the baby bird fell with a fluttery *flop*.

"Lun for your rife! I mean, *run for your life!*" squealed Brown Rabbit. He sounded like a tangled ball of yarn would sound if it could talk.

"Wait! Don't run away," Applecheek cried. "I didn't mean to scare you."

He lifted Gray Rabbit by the scruff, and set him upright. Kneeling, he scooped up the downy little bird in his cupped hands.

Brown Rabbit stopped hopping and hollering. "You didn't bare me a skit. I mean, scare me a bit. I only thought you were . . . that other boy."

Gray Rabbit added, "Yes, the one who climbed the tree and shook Downy Bird out of his nest."

Sitting in Applecheek's open hand, the bird spoke up. His voice was like wind peeping through a keyhole.

"I fell head-over tail into a clump of pink laurel. All night I hid there, and a fox nearly found me. Now I can't remember which tree I fell from. I'm lost." At that, his little beak began to quiver.

By now, I suppose you've guessed who knocked the bird out of his nest. Applecheek guessed that Ruckus did it. And even if he didn't, Ruckus got the blame.

Brown Rabbit cocked one ear thoughtfully. "The fox is sure to find Downy Bird out here in the forest. He can come and live with me—down in my burrow."

The bird shuddered. "Oh, I couldn't live under the ground."

Applecheek piped up. "I have a better idea. I'll build you a nest in the tree outside my bedroom window.

"Yes, yes. I'd like that," Downy Bird cheeped.

So they thanked the rabbits very kindly, said goodbye, and home they went.

Spring grew green and leafy into summer. In his nest, Downy Bird could hear Applecheek's mother singing as she went about her daily work.

Best of all, the boy and the bird were friends, and Applecheek no longer felt lonely. Many afternoons, they explored the rocky peaks together with Applecheek's father—up where the wild goats climbed on steep pathways.

Slowly, and day by day, the little bird was changing. His downy tufts grew into strong, stiff feathers. Applecheek was having so much fun that he never even noticed.

But Applecheek's mother saw the bird changing. One evening, she took her music book down from the shelf. "Little birds should learn to sing," she said gently.

Sitting on the cottage step, she set Downy Bird on her knee. In the evening fields, fireflies bobbed and winked. Applecheek and his father listened, and this is what she sang:

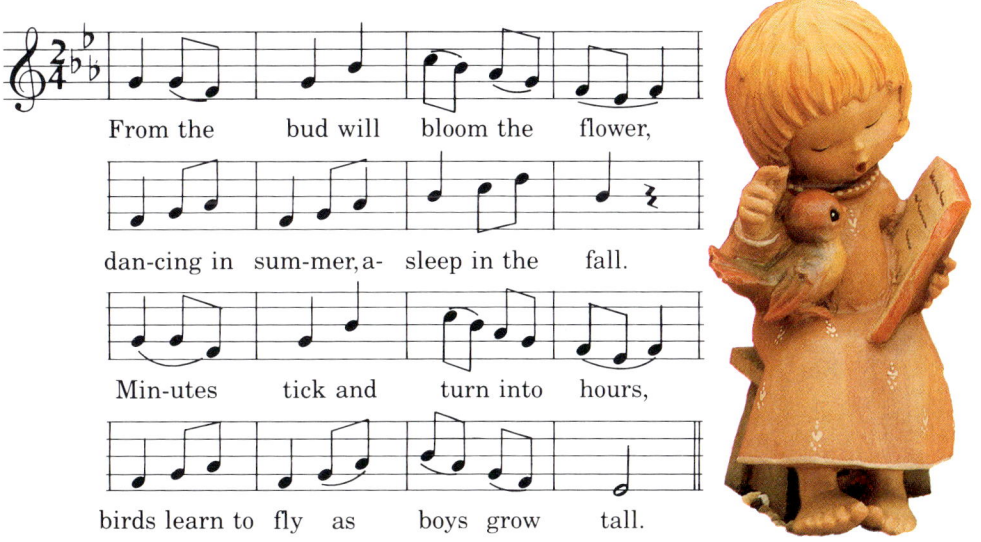

From the bud will bloom the flower,
dan-cing in sum-mer, a-sleep in the fall.
Min-utes tick and turn into hours,
birds learn to fly as boys grow tall.

When she finished, the bird said in a hushed voice, "It's a beautiful song. It makes me feel funny inside—happy and sad at the same time."

Mother smiled gently. "I believe you're growing up. You aren't a little bird any longer."

The fireflies winked sleepily in the dark fields. Applecheek was tired. He carried Downy Bird to the nest, said his prayers and hopped into bed.

The very next day, a frightening thing happened. Applecheek was hiking up the mountain, with Downy Bird perched on his shoulder. Far up the path, he spied a tall pine tree. It grew out over a ravine full of boulders that stuck up like jagged teeth.

"From the top of the tree, we can see down into the valley," Applecheek declared. "Let's climb it."

So, up they climbed, high into the windy, blue air. At the top, Applecheek clung to a prickly-thick pine branch. Down the valley, a great river curled like a question mark.

"Look," Applecheek said pointing. But that very instant, a windy gust snatched Downy Bird off his shoulder.

Down and down and down he dropped, into the rocky ravine, which hung open like a hungry mouth. As he fell, he beat his wings in fright. And what do you suppose happened then?

He stopped falling. Straight through the blue air he flew, crying, "I can fly! Look, I can fly!"

Applecheek climbed down the tree, and together they raced home to tell the glorious news.

"Flying is truly a wonderful thing to learn," said Applecheek's father. "Now you need a grown-up name. We'll call you Bright Wings."

The bird flitted his feathers. "Bright Wings," he chirped. "Yes, that's my name."

Now I wonder if you remember Ruckus, who lived beyond the oak forest? I hope that you do, for this is where he comes into the story.

Now that Bright Wings could fly, he rode the winds far down the valley each day beyond the river's question-mark curve. Each morning, Applecheek watched his friend fly away over the hills, and he felt lonely again.

Late one evening, Bright Wings was flying homeward. Below him, at the far edge of the oak forest, he saw a small cabin with warm candlelight spilling from its windows. He lighted on a windowsill, and peered inside.

Beside a wooden bed knelt Ruckus. Bright Wings shivered, remembering the day Ruckus shook him out of the nest. But now his hands were folded, and he was praying:

"Please send me a friend. No one likes me because I'm so rough. But if I had one friend to play with, I wouldn't be lonely. And maybe I'd stay out of mischief." Then he hopped into bed and blew out the candle.

The bird's heart was touched. Over the shadowy forest he flew, where the fox was hunting in the moonlight. Snuggling in his nest, Bright Wings began to hatch a plan.

Soon the trees turned red and gold and orange like flames. Leaves flew on the Autumn winds.

One chilly evening, at bedtime, Bright Wings flitted in through the open window.

"Applecheek, a voice is calling me on the wind," he chirped. "It sounds like far-off forests. Like waves of water dashing on great stones. It sounds like many wings beating together. I'm going to fly away tomorrow, before the snow and the long nights come."

The boy hung his head sadly. "You're my best friend," he murmured, as a tear slid off his cheek onto the feather quilt.

"Before I leave, I have a gift for you," the bird replied. "Meet me tomorrow morning." And saying no more, he flitted out the window into the night.

The next morning, when Applecheek awoke, Bright Wings was perched on a bare, oak branch, waiting for him.

"Hurry," he chirped. "We have a long way to go—and your gift is waiting." And off he flew through the forest.

Applecheek followed. He was red with running when the path ended at last in an open field. The sun was just peeking over a small cabin.

"But this is where Ruckus lives," Applecheek whispered. "He's a bad person. He shook you out of your nest. You don't mean for me to be *his* friend, do you?"

Bright Wings lighted on a mossy tree stump. "Applecheek," he said, "when I was little, I had a little bird's heart. But birds grow up, and so must children. I have forgiven Ruckus. Won't you forgive him, too?"

At the next, strong *swooooosh* of wind, Bright Wings rose into the air, chirping, "I've led you this far, Applecheek. But now your own heart must lead you. Goodbye . . . goodbye!" Then he was off and away on the wind.

Applecheek watched till the bird was only a speck in the sky. At last, he mustered up his courage, trudged up to the door and *knock-knock-knocked.*

Ruckus threw open the door and stared at him. Then he laughed and jumped with excitement. "My friend! My friend has come! Oh Applecheek, I'm sorry I was so mean before. But I've grown up a little, you know."

Applecheek replied, "I've grown up, too. I'm happy to be your friend."

Then Ruckus led Applecheek inside, where his mother served them eggs and hot biscuits for breakfast. Afterward, they played all day in red and gold leaves of the drowsy fall forest.

And they were best friends from then on.

When the cat finished her story the rain had passed. A few drops sparkled blue and red on the window where the sun shone through.

"I see some of your friends outside," murmured the cat. "I don't care much for puddles and wet grass myself. But you hurry along. You shouldn't spend your day indoors with an old cat."

With that she shut her eyes, and would say no more.

A SECRET TO TELL

I'm walking the cool, green-leafy lanes
and running a long, long way
with a secret inside my happy heart—
    over the hill
      under the sun—
to tell my friend today.

The little wren begs me to stop and chatter,
the billygoat skips in stride
and flowers beckon with strange perfume—
    violet, lily
      columbine—
but I must not turn aside.

My pouch may never be full of jewels
and riches I have few,
but in my heart I carry a secret—
    fine as gold
      bright as diamonds—
Shall I tell it? I love you.

A STAR IN THE NIGHT

A cold wind sighed through the stable where Prince Song was herding all the animals of the Peaceable Kingdom. The last light of day brushed the hills with gold. One star peeked in through a crack in the wooden wall as he drew a bolt across the door, and went home over the snowy meadow.

Inside, all the animals huddled against the sheep, who had the warmest wool coats. Soon they felt toasty warm.

"I have a story to tell—a true story," said the oldest ewe. "I know it's true because it happened to Fuzzle, my great, great, very great grandfather many years ago. It's about a little boy, and a star and . . . Well, I'll tell it from the beginning."

In the hills of Israel, in the sleepy town of Bethlehem, lived a boy whose name was Aaron. His family was very rich, and they lived in a mansion behind gates of solid bronze. Aaron's mother and father had once been happy and generous people who helped the poor. But something terrible happened.

From a far country, a wicked emperor sent his soldiers and horses to conquer the land of Israel. And they did.

The people of Israel were terribly angry. And the anger seemed to pierce their hearts with sharp slivers of darkness. Some grew nasty and hateful, even to their own countrymen. Only a few prayed quietly for a Deliverer—one who would drive out the soldiers and the darkness from their land.

The slivers of darkness had twisted into the hearts of Aaron's mother and father, too. They were no longer generous. Now, when the ragged men came begging bread for their children they were turned away empty-handed at the gates. Aaron's father spent silver to buy gold, and his mother traded gold for jewels. But the more they owned, the more miserable they grew.

Aaron wished with all his heart that he could bring the bright spark of joy into his parents' eyes again.

One chilly evening, Aaron was outside playing hide and seek with his little lamb named Fuzzle. The first stars were opening their eyes, and the mansion's cobbled courtyard was all shadowy.

Fuzzle covered his eyes and began counting: "One, two, three, four, five . . ." Aaron tip-toed away and hid behind a wooden rain barrel.

". . . six, seven, eight-oh *look!*" Fuzzle shouted. "Come and look, Aaron! Aaron, where are you?"

Stumbling out from behind the barrel, Aaron called, "What is it? If you've tricked me into giving out my hiding place . . ."

Fuzzle was cantering about in circles, shouting. "I saw it dance right across the sky. Oh look up! Look at the star!"

In the deep blue evening sky, a great star was shining and dancing like a jewel on a string. Silvery and mysterious, its light streamed into the courtyard.

At the same moment, a soft, low, beautiful melody drifted in from the street. Aaron and Fuzzle ran to the front gate and peered out between bronze bars. They saw nothing—but still the song drifted on the night air.

"What do you suppose is happening in Bethlehem tonight?" whispered Fuzzle.

"The emperor made a decree," Aaron replied, as the music drew nearer. "He wants everyone to be counted. People have been coming to town from all over Israel and . . ." Aaron stopped short. For just then a wonderful procession rounded the corner and came into view.

A train of camels, whose heads bobbed with each step, were led by servants in curly-toed shoes. From their swaying bundles came the glint of gold and the aroma of exotic spices. And leading the procession were three kings, their robes of jewelled satin swishing as they walked and sang:

Mysteriously

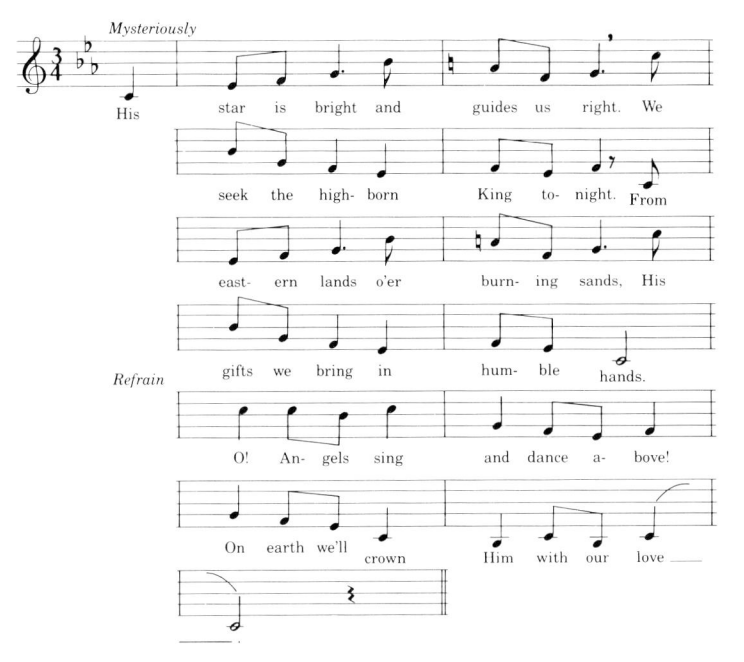

His star is bright and guides us right. We seek the high-born King to-night. From east-ern lands o'er burn-ing sands, His

Refrain

gifts we bring in hum-ble hands. O! An-gels sing and dance a-bove! On earth we'll crown Him with our love

As the last camel swayed by, something tumbled from its pack, bounced on the street and landed outside the gate. Aaron stretched his arm through the bars, but could not reach it.

"Help me open the gate, Fuzzle," he said. Together they pushed, and the gate swung slowly open, complaining on its heavy hinges.

Lying at their feet was a small, square package. It was wrapped in rich, purple satin and tied with a cord of white silk.

"Hey," Aaron called down the dark street. "You dropped something!" But by now the procession had turned a corner and disappeared from sight.

"What will you do with it?" asked Fuzzle, sniffing at the elegant box.

"I've got to find the kings and return it, of course," Aaron answered as he picked it up.

"But it's late and dark and your parents might get angry if you're out on the streets," Fuzzle said with a worried look.

Aaron paused. It was a small package—surely the kings wouldn't miss it. "I'll bet there's something wonderful inside," he mused. "But I can't keep what isn't mine. If I run, I can find the kings and still be back home before they miss me."

"Then I'll go, too," replied the lamb. And off they ran down the dark, narrow, twisting streets of Bethlehem.

The brilliant star was no longer overhead. Only once did they catch a snippet of the kings' song on the night wind. They ran faster, and peered around the next corner, but saw no one.

Out from the deep shadows stepped a man in a black hooded cloak. Aaron and Fuzzle trembled as he came closer.

"Oho! What are you doing out so late?" the man laughed. His dark eyes flashed inside his hood. "What's in your package? Could it be a gift—for the prince of thieves?"

The thief leaped at them. Aaron and Fuzzle fled in terror through the town. They spun around corners and stumbled on stones till they fell in a breathless heap. But the thief did not chase them.

"Let's go home," Fuzzle panted.

Aaron sat clutching the package. What was inside it? He was about to speak when he heard laughter and loud talking. At the far end of the street, noisy voices and firelight spilled from the village inn.

"I'll bet the kings are staying at the inn," he said, leaping to his feet.

When they knocked at the door, the fat innkeeper thrust his round face out at them. "No room here," he grunted. "Go away!"

"Please, sir," Aaron begged. "We're looking for three kings and . . ."

"Kings?" snarled the innkeeper, and his jowls jiggled. "My inn is full with travelers. I've been turnin' folks away all night—and those what's inside are yammerin' for food and clean beds. Now you shows up botherin' me with nonsense. It's more than a body can take."

From inside, someone called, "Innkeeper! Another chicken leg! And some of us haven't had our pie!"

The innkeeper growled, "Go home and quit pesterin' folks." And the door slammed with a nasty wooden bite.

Fuzzle's woolly tail drooped as they trudged down the silent streets. Suddenly, a voice startled them.

"I will take you to the King!" At the end of a black alleyway, a lantern bobbed and glowed, but they could not see who was speaking.

"We're looking for *three* kings," Aaron replied timidly.

From behind the lantern, the voice chuckled. "There is only one true King. I was sent to guide you safely to Him."

With that, the lantern bobbed off through the night. Aaron and Fuzzle had no choice but to follow the unseen guide. They were very confused now, but strangely unafraid.

The lantern led them out to the edge of town, right up to an old stable. There was the star again, gleaming in the sky directly overhead. They stopped at the stable door, and the mysterious lantern-bearer declared: "The King is within!"

The wooden door opened just a peek. Aaron and Fuzzle peered in cautiously. Such a sight greeted them!

The stable was not a stable at all, but a throne room glittering in silver and gold. Courtiers in brocade and velvet waistcoats stood beside ladies in flowing gowns. In the center of the marble floor knelt the three kings. They were bowing to the most radiant young Lord! Light burst from His throne, and His laughter rang to the very stars of heaven.

Aaron drew his head out and whispered, "But He has no crown."

The invisible lantern-bearer opened the door wider and said, "That is why you have come."

When Aaron and Fuzzle stepped inside they were astonished.

The marble throne room was gone. Starlight shone pale through a crack in the wooden walls. A young mother was singing softly to her newborn baby, who lay cooing and smiling in a manger of straw. Leaning on a crooked staff was the woman's husband. Only the three kings looked the same. They were kneeling still—not on marble, but on straw.

Aaron tugged gently at the robe of the oldest king. "Excuse me," he stammered, holding out the beautiful little box. "I've come to return this—it fell from one of your camels."

"Bless me!" cried the old king, hobbling to his feet. He clapped the youngest king on the back and chortled, "This boy has found our special gift, Balthazar. And you thought I'd forgotten to pack it. Oh, thank you, wonderful prince of a boy!"

Aaron sighed. "I just don't understand what's happening tonight. When we first looked in the door, we saw a royal court, with gentlemen and ladies. And the baby was a High King with light gleaming from his throne. And—and now . . ." he faltered.

The youngest king stood up. "Perhaps the starlight tricked your eyes. The baby *is* a King—though His court is but a poor stable, as you see."

Aaron looked about. In one corner lay sheep and a few rabbits that had crept in from the forest. Some ragged shepherd children played soft music on pipes and flutes. Next to them lay an ox, blinking his brown, gentle eyes.

Then the black king, whose name was Melchior, spoke. His voice was rich and deep like chocolate melting into cocoa. "A young king has much to learn, Balthazar. It is plain that God has given this lad a pure heart. The Spirit of truth and honesty has guided him here."

Turning to Aaron he said, "Tonight your eyes have seen what is true. This *is* the court of the Most High King—the Son of God! Beggars, shepherds or kings, we are all His royal subjects." And pointing to the package he announced: "You shall give the King His special gift."

Aaron knelt quietly beside the baby's crib and placed the gift in the young mother's lap.

"Thank you," said Mary and Joseph together. The silk and purple satin unwound in Mary's hands, and she lifted from the box a tiny, jewelled crown. Carved into the gold were the words: KING OF KINGS.

Time held its breath. The children played soft music, and outside the star burned brightly. Fuzzle lay at the foot of the manger-bed, nuzzling the baby's foot. And the baby—the Lord Jesus—cooed and held His crown in tiny hands.

All at once, Aaron jumped to his feet. "Oh, I forgot about mother and father. They'll be angry that I'm out so late. Come on Fuzzle. Goodbye, everyone. Goodbye!" And he rushed for the door with the lamb stumbling at his heels.

Outside, the bobbing lantern halted them. "The King also has a gift for you. You must not leave without it," said the guide. And suddenly the lantern's glow was swallowed in the white light of a radiant winged angel.

The angel rose into the air. "Good men will shine as the stars forever—and so will good children. They bring joy to the whole earth." From the velvety sky, he plucked three stars and let them drop.

Aaron reached out and caught the falling stars. They buzzed and tickled in his hand.

"Thank you. Thank you very much," Aaron called to the angel. "Hurry, Fuzzle. Let's take these to mother and father."

But as they ran through Bethlehem, the stars melted in Aaron's hand. When he reached the bronze gate, there was only a faint glow left in his palm.

"They'll never believe me now, Fuzzle," said Aaron. But he felt all happy inside, not at all worried.

Aaron found his mother and father sitting in the great hall, and the wondrous story tumbled out.

"Fuzzle and I saw three kings. And a baby in a stable—He was the Most High King, the Son of God. He gave me three stars—only they melted!"

His mother and father listened quietly. As Aaron spoke, a marvelous change began. A look of peace crossed his father's face. "Aaron," he whispered dreamily, "a warm light is shining from your eyes."

"Yes," added his mother. "It makes me all—joyful! I used to feel cold inside. But now I'm starting to feel warm and happy again. It feels good!" And she began laughing.

"Tomorrow, we will have a feast," his parents announced. "And all the poor people of Bethlehem will be guests of honor."

They hugged Aaron tightly, laughing as the last chilly sliver of darkness melted from their hearts.

UNDER GOD'S CANOPY

Under God's canopy of soft night sky
   the world's eyes are drowsy and the stars wheel by
   as Mother fluffs the pillow for my sleepy head
   and Father whispers prayers with me—now, into bed!

Rings of winging angels guide me in my dreams
   in a peaceful land of golden fields and singing streams,
   where flowers push away the thorns, the crooked path unbends,
   the lion and the lamb curl up in peace as friends,

where nations lay their guns aside, no blood is shed,
   the poor are rich, the sick are whole, the hungry fed,
   and children wake to find the sun is sweeping high
   under God's canopy of bright new sky.